B]

AND THE
FIRST FLAG
OF THE
UNITED STATES
OF AMERICA

*The People, Events, and Ideas Behind
the Design and Creation of the Flag and
Seal of the United States*

Col. J. Franklin Reigart

Addie Guthrie Weaver

Edited by *Anthony R. Michalski*

www. **ALLISTI**publishing.com

www.KallistiPublishing.com

Betsy Ross and the First Flag of the United States of America: The People, Events, and Ideas Behind the Design and Creation of the Flag and Seal of the United States. © 2019 by Anthony R. Michalski. All rights reserved. No part of this book may be reproduced, in any form, without written permission from the publisher.

This book is an edited and abridged anthology of *The Story of Our Flag* by Addie Guthrie Weaver (1898) and *The History of the First United States Flag* by Col. J. Franklin Reigart (1878).

ISBN-13 978-0-9848162-8-6

Library of Congress Control Number: 2019948203

Kallisti Publishing makes personal development and business books that expand the mind, generate ideas, and grow profits. A book from Kallisti Publishing informs, inspires, and impels. Kallisti Publishing sells traditional books and ebooks through distributors and retailers, through its own affiliate network, direct to the reader, and in bulk to companies and organizations. Please contact Kallisti Publishing for more information at *www.kallistipublishing.com/resources/bulk-sales/*.

Kallisti Publishing and its logo are trademarks of Kallisti Publishing. All rights reserved.

Book and cover design by *AnthonyRaymond.com*.

This book is set in *ITC Caslon 224*.

The About US book series

Please note that any errors, typographical or otherwise, are here for a purpose: some people actually enjoy looking for them and we strive to please as many readers as possible. If you should find any errors, please contact us via our web site— *www.kallistipublishing.com/resources/report-a-typo/*.

CONTENTS

PREFACE

824, WHEN GENERAL LAFAYETTE ARRIVED AT
adelphia, and was nobly welcomed as "The
on's Guest," the writer of this book was stay-
several weeks at the hospitable home of his
able and kind relative, Mrs. Betsy Ross. The
al of Lafayette excited and brightened her
aordinary memory, as she very cheerfully
rtained all her friends, by relating the most
resting facts of the Revolution, and its Flag
ictory. Her words we well remember. She ob-
ed, as a member of the society of "Friends,"
t for her portrait; nevertheless, a miniature
er in crayon was made, and is now highly
ed; and at this late day, we deem it our duty
ublish the true history of the origin of the
flag of our country, and the patriotism of
erica's most illustrious heroine.

The bravest of the brave demands
our song,
Who made the Flag so firm and
strong,
Of all earth's emblems the brightest
diadem,
The Freemen's shield, the Patriot's
gem.

Listen to her thrilling, cheering voice, her
-inspiring, martial song, whilst a dozen of
ladies of her household joined in the cho-

INTRODUCTION

A COUNTRY IS COMPOSED OF PEOPLE SITUATED ON A PIECE
of land who share some basic traits—language, mores, and customs. Later, those people forge a nation
and it adopts symbols that serve as identifiers of
their beliefs, laws, and aspirations.

No symbol of any sovereign nation is more telling, nor more high, than its flag. It is carried into
battle and waved during peacetime. It bedecks halls
of justice and watches over public lands. A man will
doff his hat for it and all will raise their head for it.

Of all secular symbols, a nation's flag is the most
sacred—and no flag has been as esteemed as the
flag of the United States of America. It symbolizes freedom, bravery, justice, and hope to people
around the world, citizen of this great land or not.

A nation's flag not only tells a story, it *has* a
story. The story of one Betsy Ross and the creation
of the American flag is an exceptional one. In this
first book of the *About U.S.* series, you will thrill at
the description of her creative design and then read
agog as the Founding Fathers, guided by the Stars
and Stripes, forge a nation that would secure freedom and happiness for all—and would continue to
do so to this very day.

Long may it wave o'er these hallowed lands!

And may God continue the bless us with life,
liberty, and the pursuit of happiness.

Anthony R. Michalski
Editor

A nation thrills, a nation bleeds,
A nation follows where it leads,
And every man is proud to yield
His life upon a crimson field
For Betsy's battle flag.

— *Minna Irving,*
from "Betsy's Battle Flag"

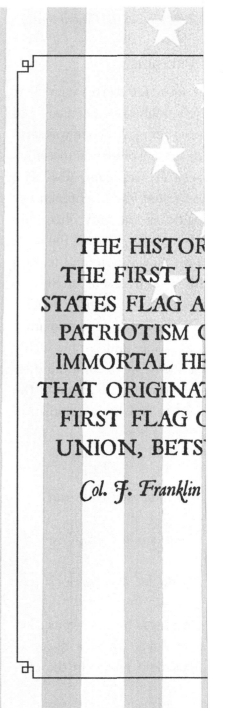

THE HISTOR
THE FIRST U
STATES FLAG A
PATRIOTISM (
IMMORTAL HE
THAT ORIGINA
FIRST FLAG (
UNION, BETS

Col. J. Franklin

rus, as she handed over each Flag to the gallant troops, on their way to camp, and roused their enthusiasm to the highest pitch. The ladies of the Revolution loved her for her magnanimous and modest Quaker deportment, and the army of Washington applauded her dignified admonitions, so full of patriotism and power of song. Quakers very seldom sing, but Betsy Ross always said, *"My voice shall be devoted to God and my country, and whenever the spirit moves me, I'll sing and shout for liberty!"* And with an enthusiasm for Independence, exhibiting a spirit power, only to be equalled by absolute phrensy, she waved her Flag aloft, and she did sing to the gallant volunteers, the "War Song of Independence."

> *Come on, my hearts of temper'd steel,*
> *Away! away! to arms!!*
> *No foreign slaves shall give us law,*
> *No British tyrants reign;*
> *'Tis Independence makes us free,*
> *And Freedom we'll maintain.*
> > *And to conquest we will go! will go! will go!*
> > *With the red, white and blue,*
> > *To conquest we will go.*
> *A soldier is a gentleman,*

His honor is his life,
And he that won't stand by his Flag,
Will ne'er stand by his Wife.

> *And to conquest we will*
> *go! will go! will go!*
> *With the red, white and*
> *blue,*
> *To conquest we will go.*

Then hark! to arms! to arms!! to
arms!!!
'Tis the time that tries men's souls!
The rising world shall sing of you,
A Thousand Years to come,
And to your children's children
TELL
The Wonders you have done.

> *When to conquest you did*
> *go! did go! did go!*
> *With the red, white and*
> *blue,*
> *To conquest you did go.*

Many inspired songs (after the close of the war for American Independence) were carried home by Gen. Lafayette, (the companion of Washington,) Rochambeau, and many of the French engineers and soldiers, on their return to France, having proved their chivalry and united their hearts, blood, songs and arms with Americans, for the liberties of America; and, but for

INTRODUCTION

A COUNTRY IS COMPOSED OF PEOPLE SITUATED ON A PIECE of land who share some basic traits—language, mores, and customs. Later, those people forge a nation and it adopts symbols that serve as identifiers of their beliefs, laws, and aspirations.

No symbol of any sovereign nation is more telling, nor more high, than its flag. It is carried into battle and waved during peacetime. It bedecks halls of justice and watches over public lands. A man will doff his hat for it and all will raise their head for it.

Of all secular symbols, a nation's flag is the most sacred—and no flag has been as esteemed as the flag of the United States of America. It symbolizes freedom, bravery, justice, and hope to people around the world, citizen of this great land or not.

A nation's flag not only tells a story, it *has* a story. The story of one Betsy Ross and the creation of the American flag is an exceptional one. In this first book of the *About U.S.* series, you will thrill at the description of her creative design and then read agog as the Founding Fathers, guided by the Stars and Stripes, forge a nation that would secure freedom and happiness for all—and would continue to do so to this very day.

Long may it wave o'er these hallowed lands!

And may God continue the bless us with life, liberty, and the pursuit of happiness.

Anthony R. Michalski
Editor

A nation thrills, a nation bleeds,
A nation follows where it leads,
And every man is proud to yield
His life upon a crimson field
For Betsy's battle flag.

— Minna Irving,
from "Betsy's Battle Flag"

THE HISTORY OF THE FIRST UNITED STATES FLAG AND THE PATRIOTISM OF THE IMMORTAL HEROINE THAT ORIGINATED THE FIRST FLAG OF THE UNION, BETSY ROSS

Col. J. Franklin Reigart

PREFACE

IN 1824, WHEN GENERAL LAFAYETTE ARRIVED AT Philadelphia, and was nobly welcomed as "The Nation's Guest," the writer of this book was staying several weeks at the hospitable home of his amiable and kind relative, Mrs. Betsy Ross. The arrival of Lafayette excited and brightened her extraordinary memory, as she very cheerfully entertained all her friends, by relating the most interesting facts of the Revolution, and its Flag of Victory. Her words we well remember. She objected, as a member of the society of "Friends," to sit for her portrait; nevertheless, a miniature of her in crayon was made, and is now highly prized; and at this late day, we deem it our duty to publish the true history of the origin of the first flag of our country, and the patriotism of America's most illustrious heroine.

> *The bravest of the brave demands our song,*
> *Who made the Flag so firm and strong,*
> *Of all earth's emblems the brightest diadem,*
> *The Freemen's shield, the Patriot's gem.*

Listen to her thrilling, cheering voice, her soul-inspiring, martial song, whilst a dozen of the ladies of her household joined in the cho-

"Quakers," she invariably used cloths of the very brightest, and in every instance the primary colors combined, so as to be distinguished from all other objects, and she quickly judged and comprehended the styles that would best please her customers. Her brilliant draperies and tri-colored curtains, in the public halls, hotel parlors, and drawing rooms, were greatly admired; whilst General Washington, General Hand, Thomas Mifflin, George Clymer, Jared Ingersoll, J. Koch, Gouveneur Morris, Robert Morris, Judge James Wilson, Frederick A. Muhlenberg, Joseph Wilson, Caleb and Thomas Cope, Thomas Wilson, Timothy Matlack, James Trimble, and William Shippen, are some of the names on her storebooks, as her generous and kind friends and patrons, whose heirs still possess beautiful curtains and magnificent quilts of variegated silks and satins, unsurpassed, at this day, for beauty of utility, justness of composition, that none but a perfect artist could produce; and the constant use of materials of primary colors were her praise, excellence, and fame.

Colonel George Ross, (a member of the Continental Congress,) and James Trimble, (afterwards Deputy Secretary of Pennsylvania,) were her brothers-in-law, and through their suggestions, she adorned, with drapery, the Hall of Congress, and the Governor's reception room.

Her upholstery in the ladies' cabins and state
rooms of Caleb and Thomas Cope's packet ships
was unrivalled and not equalled by the state
rooms of the European packets; whilst from
the topmasts of Cope's packets, her waving red,
white, and blue streamers made glad the trav-
elers of the seas, several years before the Revolution of 1776. Some of the theatres and public halls of Philadelphia were embellished and
decorated with curtains of white, mazarine, and
scarlet velvets and silks in waves, festoons, and
pendents, and in many instances the curtains
were embroidered with gold and silver figures
of vines, leaves, and stars that glittered with su-
perb brilliancy, whilst the curtains were invariably supported by a golden spread eagle, with
lightning darts in its talons and a silvery olive
branch in its beak; and these were the original
and wonderful handiwork of Betsy Ross. She
could not think of or invent anything brighter
or more graceful than her most celebrated gay
and glittering primary colored curtains, spangled with stars and supported by a golden eagle, that already ornamented and adorned the
interior of the chief Halls of the land. They were
her daily delight and divinely brilliant dreams
by night. With her scissors she cut the form of a
small shield, upon which she sewed five-pointed stars and tri-colored stripes, in imitation of

General Washington's coat-of-arms, which embraced stars and pales upon his escutcheon; this shield she fastened upon the eagle's breast; and, inspired with one bright thought, she seized her meritorious daily work, flung it to the breeze, hung it "upon the outer walls" and the Freemen of Columbia cheered, and hailed it "The Flag of the Union!" And that one independent fling made all the people King!

At the request of Dr. Franklin, Mr. Robert Morris and Col. George Ross, she designed and made the first Flag of the United States, consisting of thirteen red and white stripes, a blue field as a square, on the left and upper corner, and upon the blue field was a spread eagle, with thirteen stars, in a circle of rays of glory, surrounding its head, and the United States Seal was afterwards made from the same design of the United States Flag, *viz:* A red, white and blue shield on the breast of an American Eagle, holding in its talons an olive branch and thirteen arrows; in its beak a scroll inscribed with this motto, *"E Pluribus Unum,"* and above its head thirteen stars arranged in a circle of glory. These designs were approved and adopted by the Committee and Congress, and they were made before the words "United States of America," were legally used. The country was called "Columbia," the Congress was styled the

"Continental Congress," the States were called "Colonies"; every petition sent to the King of Great Britain, and every public document, were issued by "The North American Colonies"; our Country had no name until Betsy Ross marked upon her Flags, "The United States of America." Dr. Franklin, John Adams and Thomas Jefferson had been appointed (December, 1775, by Congress, a Secret Committee) to prepare a flag, and a device for a Seal for the Colonies, and Dr. Rittenhouse was requested by the Committee, to engrave the Seal corresponding with the eagle on the Flag.

On the 4th day of July, 1776, the Declaration of Independence was finished and signed, and the Rev. Dr. Duché, Chaplain of Congress, had offered up his celebrated "Prayer of Independence," the Star Spangled Banner was unfurled, and emblazoned the Hall of Independence, and hung around the spire of the Old State House Bell, as it sounded its tones of warning beyond the city limits, re-echoed across the Delaware, and proclaimed the liberty of the land, amidst the thundering shouts of Freemen, the roaring of cannons, musketry, firearms, and bonfires; then the Secret Committee, Franklin, Jefferson and Adams, was publicly announced by the President of Congress, and the Seal (already made) of the "United Colonies," was used that day. Aye!

the Flags waved, the Seal was engraved, and the thirteen "United States of America" were saved.

The Flag was afterwards adopted by Congress, June 14, 1777, and September 15, 1789, they passed the act, that "The Seal heretofore used by the 'United Colonies' in Congress assembled, shall be the Seal of the 'United States;'" and for his beautiful workmanship in engraving that seal, Dr. Rittenhouse was honored with the appointment of Director of the United States Mint; and Franklin styled Rittenhouse, "the Newton of America."

Mrs. Ross also engaged Mr. George Barrett, (of Cherry near Third street, Philadelphia,) an ornamental painter, and accomplished artist, to paint upon the blue fields of one dozen silk Flags, a gilded bald-headed spread eagle, with thirteen silvered stars encircling its head in rays of glory, which were executed in the finest artistic style, for the use of Congress and General Washington's army; they were always much admired, and daily used until worn out; and, Betsy Ross also directed Mr. Barrett to ornament the army drums with the same design of the eagle and thirteen stars, and the letters "United States of America," that gave great delight and spirit to the drummers, to such an extent that Mr. Barrett was kept busy ornamenting flags, flagstaffs, and drums for Washington's army. The committee of Congress were so much pleased with the design of the eagle and thirteen stars that they concluded to adopt and use it for the "National Seal" exclusively; but, Betsy Ross, Col. George Ross, and Lieut. Paul Jones earnestly protested against despoiling the Flag by leaving out and omitting the eagle, and declared that the Army might, if they choose, have the stars only, but as for the Navy they would never give up the Bald Eagle, the conquerer of all birds, belonging only to America; and from that day to this the bald eagle of America spreads its wings upon the Flags of the United States Revenue vessels as the emblem of freedom, independence, liberty, power, empire, and victory.

From that time our beautiful Flag was composed of thirteen stars and stripes. The red stripes were emblematic of fervency and zeal; the white, of integrity and purity; the blue field with stars, of unity, power, and glory. The number thirteen was symbolical of the thirteen colonial states, that severed their allegiance from the sovereignty of Great Britain, and declared, in 1776, that they were free and independent powers.

The size of the Flag of the army is six feet six inches in length, by four feet four inches in width, with seven red and six white stripes. The first seven stripes, (four red and three white,) bound the square of the blue field for the stars, the stripes extending from the extremity of the field to the end of the Flag. The eighth stripe is white, extending partly at the base of the field.

According to the act of Congress, April 4, 1818, on the admission of every new State into the Union, a star was to be added to the galaxy of the most brilliant banner of earth.

Mrs. Betsy Ross put all her household to work in earnest, and the "Flags," made of silk and bunting, were not only admired, but afterwards approved and adopted by the committee of Congress. General George Washington, Dr. Benjamin Franklin, and Thomas Jefferson, frequently visited her store, to see what progress she was making, and were not only pleased, but expressed their astonishment at her dexterity and judgment, and in the most flattering terms complimented her for her remarkable skill with the SCISSORS, as she folded a piece of white silk and with one cut formed the beautiful five-pointed star.

Mrs. Ross, by order of the Government, continued making the army and navy Flags of the United States for upwards of fifty-five years, and after her death, in 1832, her daughter, Mrs. Clarissa S. Wilson continued the business, and they became generally and widely known as the most patriotic ladies of America. After the death of Mr. John Ross, she was married to Mr. John Claypoole, the grandson of Sir John Claypoole, the grandson of Oliver Cromwell, who came to Philadelphia with William Penn. She afterwards moved from Arch near Third street, to Second street near Dock, where she resided until her death, at the good old age of four score years and ten.

Mrs. Betsy Ross was of medium height, strong in form, but remarkably graceful and erect; she had a handsome face, a very fair transparent complexion, projecting eyebrows, blue sparkling eyes, and light brown hair. She was a perfect "Friend" in all her speech and movements; possessed of the most refined sprightly intellect and polished education; in fact she was well known throughout the whole of Philadelphia city, as a "sharp, thorough going woman." First in Friends' Meeting, where the spirit moved her to speak and to act; First amidst the Daughters of Benevolence, furnishing clothing and lint for the Continental troops, scattering printed patriotic songs and appeals amongst them; and First and most effective in her attentions to the sick. She was, in truth, what her friends styled her, "A Healing Medium,"—but respected and esteemed by all the physicians and surgeons of Philadelphia, as "the true Friend of the sick," for when her hand touched and bathed the burning fevered brow of the sick soldier, he knew that he had one friend, and that friend was a true one. Whenever she entered the sick chamber, she saturated her handkerchief with vinegar, (that she carried in a phial in her pocket, as a precaution against contagion) and after wiping her forehead, lips and hands, she quietly approached the bedside of the afflicted invalid, and placing her hand upon his forehead, she would whisper these words, "In the name of the Lord Jesus Christ, I pray that your health may be restored," and then she would administer the medicines and restoratives as directed by the visiting physicians; and her angelic nature, purer than that of Jeanne Dare, was the powerful agency of health. She was the worthiest Heroine of the Revolution.

During the frightful devastation caused by the yellow fever in 1793, Mrs. Betsy Ross was most active in alleviating the terrible miseries of that epidemic. Moved with sorrow at the sufferings of others, she carried not only her own life in her hands, but medicines to relieve the sick and dying. Day and night she ceased not; whilst her angelic visits were cheered with success. Her personal perfections irresistably commanded the admiration and love of the sick and afflicted to such a degree, that the celebrated Dr. Benjamin Rush, styled her the "Magical Quakeress."

They who would not now honor, esteem, and love the name of Betsy Ross do not deserve to enjoy the protection of the glorious starry Flag of the Union, in the land of the free and home of the brave, or in any land upon earth where the Flag of the Union waves. Her biography will ornament the brightest pages of our country's history, and her statue, surrounded by a group of her daughters and nieces, cutting, sewing and making the "Star Spangled Banners," must soon grace the Capitol of our nation, and the patriotic Ladies of America will design, erect, and pay for it. Yes, the friend of Washington, Franklin, Adams, Jefferson, Morris, Jones, Rittenhouse, Ross, the immutable friend of Liberty, and of the soldiers of the Independence of 1776, will forever live in the hearts of all freemen.

JOHN PAUL JONES
WITH THE FIRST U.S. FLAG ESTABLISHES THE FREEDOM OF THE SEAS

JOHN PAUL JONES, THE BRAVEST OF NAVAL COM-manders, was born at Selkirk, Scotland, 1730, and came to America about 1770, to fight the battles of Liberty and Independence. He was styled "The Washington of the Seas," "The deadliest foe of Cowards." Lieutenant Paul Jones and Mrs. Elizabeth Ross, of Philadelphia, became intimate friends and neighbors, well known as the most zealous patriots in the cause of Independence, doing battle against tyrants and oppressors, and Thomas Jefferson, Dr. Franklin, John Adams, Dr. Rittenhouse and Robert Morris were their truest and most steadfast friends and patrons. Mrs. Ross designed and made the Flag that Lieutenant Jones hoisted upon the Flagship of War, in the Delaware bay. During the month of December, 1775, by the request and explicit orders of Dr. Franklin, Col. George Ross and Robert Morris, the three members of a Secret Committee of Congress, Lieutenant Jones was supplied with one of Mrs. Ross' first and best Flags, the red white and blue emblem of Liberty, for which Congress paid. Afterward, for Jones' brave honoring of that Flag, Congress awarded him $25,000 and a golden medal, and he was further complimented by an invitation to Paris, where the cross of military merit and a sword of honor were presented to him by the King of France, at the written request of our Congress, for his dauntless courage and his triumphant victory as the Captain of the *Richard*, with the first Flag of the Union, over the British Flag of the *Serapis*.

In January 1776, the following vessels were fitted out.

The *Alfred*, of thirty guns and three hundred men, Dudley Saltonstall, Captain, bearing the

Pine Tree Flag, presented by the colony of Connecticut.

The *Columbus*, of twenty-eight guns and three hundred men, Abraham Whipple, Captain, bearing the Flag of the Red Cross of Saint George, presented by the Colony of Vermont.

The *Andrew Doria*, of eighteen guns and two hundred men, Nicholas Biddle, Captain, bearing the Flag of the White Cross of Saint Andrew, presented by the Philadelphians.

The *Cabot*, of fourteen guns and two hundred men, John W. Hopkins, Captain, bearing the Pine Tree white silk Flag from Connecticut.

The *Providence*, of twelve guns, bearing the Flag with the Cross of Saint Andrew, presented by Rhode Island.

The *Hornet*, of fourteen guns, bearing the yellow silk Flag of Virginia, with Rattlesnake.

The *Wasp*, eight guns, bearing the yellow silk Flag of South Carolina, with a Crescent, a Beaver and a Rattlesnake, with the motto, "Don't tread on me."

The Dispatch vessel *Fly*, bearing a blue Flag with Red Cross of Saint George.

E. Hopkins, was Commander-in-chief of the fleet, and John Paul Jones first lieutenant. Jones was offered the command of the sloop *Providence*, which he declined, declaring that he preferred to be "Chevalier Bannaret," to hoist and carry the bald eagle, with glittering stars and stripes, on the flagship *Alfred*, and when the Commander-in-chief, E. Hopkins, came on board of her, January 1, 1776, Jones hoisted the American Union Flag, with his own hands, which was the first time it was ever displayed on a man-of-war, and waving his navy cap swiftly overhead, shouted, "Three Cheers for the Red, White and Blue! The Haughtiest of Monarchs shall bow before that Flag!!! Again, Three cheers for our Commander-in-Chief and the American Navy!!!" And thus he boldly evinced his lofty and chivalrous character, bravely assuming the responsibility, and his achievement of glorious deeds aided in the recognition of our Independence.

On the 14th day of February, 1778, the United States Flag was, for the first time, recognized in the fullest and completest manner by the Flag of France. Lieutenant Paul Jones, on board the brig *Independence*, at the entrance of Quiberon bay, sailed through the French fleet, commanded by Admiral La Motte Piquet, (who was keeping the coast of France clear of British cruisers,) and our National Emblem was most courteously complimented and saluted by nine guns. The American Flag was first carried around the world in 1789, by the *Columbia*, Captain Gray, of Boston, and saluted in every port.

THE COLONY REBEL FLAGS

PRIOR TO JULY 4TH, **1776**, VARIOUS KINDS OF FLAGS were used. Mr. Endicott, Puritan Governor, aided in a religious crusade against the cross of St. George; he cut the cross from the flag flying at Salem, and was tried for treason, but escaped on the ground that his act was not actuated by treasonable motives, but religious zeal.

About the first of January, 1776, the immortal Washington unfurled his Flag in compliment to the United Colonies, but it was so nearly like the British Flag, that the Bunker Hill patriots objected to it, because it was a blue Flag with the St. George and St. Andrew's crosses combined; too much like the Flag of the Britons. Nearly every regiment had its own colony Flag. All sorts of devices, corresponding with the variegated coats of the Continental troops, or militia, scarcely two alike. They were styled "Colony Rebel Flags." Still, the "Colony Rebel Flags" were all used as rallying flags, until they were eclipsed by the starry flag, called "The Appeal to Heaven"—"The Star Spangled Banner."

WASHINGTON'S ORDER
FOR "THE FLAG OF THE UNION"

TO GENERAL PUTNAM, DESIRING HIM IN THE MOST pressing terms, to give positive orders to all the Colonels to have "Union Colors" immediately completed for their respective regiments; and Colonel Kitzema received the two first regimental silk "stars and stripes" from the secret committee of Congress, through General Putnam, and Colonel Curtenieus; whilst the brilliant Banner of the Union floated from the top of Washington's headquarters in New York City.

The real truth was, that previous to the "Declaration of Independence," the leaders of our armies, the Governors of the thirteen colonies, and the Continental Congress were afraid to publicly unfurl an Independent Union Flag; even Washington's combined crosses were discountenanced, disapproved of, and treated with indifference; but, the boldness of Colonel George Ross and John Ross, with the dashing, daring seamanship of Paul Jones, the firm patriotism, industry, and energy of that devoted friend of Independence, the Immortal Betsy Ross, who forced the "Flag of Liberty" forward, as true patriots of America, bid defiance to all Tory opposition, and flaunted the Stars and Stripes from the highest pinnacles of our land, the "Union Standard," that was never styled a "Rebel Flag," or Flag of any single Colony or State, but was styled "The Appeal to Heaven," made the cherished Flag of Independence, the triumphant Flag of Earth!

THE RATTLESNAKE FLAG OF 1775
THAT CHARMED AND INCITED THE TROOPS OF VIRGINIA TO ACTION

THE FLAG OF VIRGINIA WAS A RATTLESNAKE WITH BLUE tongue forked like lightning, and with thirteen rattles, looking like a fierce Anaconda coiled, but with head and tail up, painted on white silk, having the motto, "Don't tread on me!" It was considered as an emblem of wisdom, and of endless duration as a representative of America, an animal found in no other part of the world. The eye of this creature excels in brightness that of any other animal; it has no eyelids and is therefore an emblem of vigilance. It never begins an attack nor ever surrenders, it is therefore an emblem of magnanimity and true courage. It never wounds until it has given notice to its enemies of their danger. Its wounds, however small, are decisive and fatal. The power of fascination attributed to it resembles America. Those who look steadily in its eyes are delighted, and involuntarily advance toward, and having once approached it, never leave it.

THE FLAG AT YORKTOWN

AT THE BATTLE OF YORKTOWN, OCTOBER 19, 1781, the French troops triumphantly carried our American Stars and Stripes, with the spread eagle on the blue field, for the eagle was their adoration, and they stormed the redoubts, led on by the chivalric and heroic Generals Muhlenberg and Lafayette, who immediately hoisted that Flag upon the turret of the fortifications. The instant that Lord Cornwallis spied it, he was terror stricken. The waving of that Flag compelled him to surrender; for that Flag was the proclamation of Victory! and it ended the war in a blaze of glory.

THE FLAG WITH ITS MESSAGE

WHEREVER THE FLAG OF BETSY ROSS WENT, IT WAVED majestically and above suspicion; no temptation or opposition could deter it, for her godly prayer went with it, and upon every Flag she forwarded, she pinned her printed message, viz: "Every man that is against this Flag is a Traitor." Aye! where the battle was the hottest, and amidst the hail of fire where the bullets fell the fastest and thickest, that Flag cheered the wounded and dying patriots to shout "Fight on! Fight on! Fight on!" And when the brave Commander Lawrence saw that the Flag on his Frigate still waved, though wounded and dying, he cried out, in these immortal words, "Don't give up the ship!"

On the 28th of June, 1776, the British Fleet and Army of Sir Henry Clinton commenced their furious "Attack on Fort Moultrie," but, one circumstance serves to illustrate the daring, en-

thusiastic courage and love for the Flag of Independence which pervaded the American Troops.
In the course of the engagement, the Flag staff of
the Fort was shot away, followed by peals of derision from the minions of the Fleet, but Sergeant
Jasper leaped down upon the beach, snatched
up the Flag, fastened it to a sponge-staff, and
while the ships were incessantly directing their
broadsides upon the Fort, he mounted the mer-
lon and deliberately replaced the Flag, shouting
"It still flies!" That warrior's shout was echoed
by the Garrison, and suddenly checked Sir Henry's derision. The British Fleet and Army were
greatly mortified by the flying Stars and Stripes,
and were terribly repulsed by the brave defence
of Fort Moultrie, whilst the whole Garrison were
fiercely echoing and re-echoing the shout—"IT
STILL FLIES!!" The news of this undaunted in-
trepidity and exulting victory spread throughout
the continent, and Sergeant Jasper was honor-
ably promoted by Congress for his unparalleled
heroism. Yes, thank God, our Flag "IT STILL
FLIES"—and never can be conquered.

THE CENTENNIAL FLAG

AT THE CENTENNIAL CELEBRATION AND WORLD'S EX-
hibition at the city of Philadelphia, 1876, "The
Flags of all Nations" waved from the highest
pinnacles, but the flashing, glittering "Star

Spangled Banner" far outshone them all; like a
mighty flame of Liberty flying through the skies,
it blazed and waved, streamed and flew as the
victorious Starry Banner of the Firmament, proclaiming by its expanding, snapping, cracking,
sharper, louder sounds, the establishment of
Freedom, Liberty, Independence, and the Union
of the World! whilst in every house its graceful
folds protected each and all in their own religious, family worship; the household Idol of
Peace that ever and anon, silently wafted every
daily prayer and song of praise, to the God of
our Fathers, the true and holy Creator of the
Universe.

PATRIOTIC SONGS

THE FOLLOWING ARE COPIES OF SOME OF THE PRINTED
Songs and Appeals that Betsy Ross circulat-
ed and distributed with her own hands in the
streets of Philadelphia, and from the front door
of her Flag store and depot, to the troops on
their way to Washington's camp:

"The Gallant Volunteer of 1776"

*Come on, my hearts of temper'd
steel,*

And leave your girls and farms,
*Your sports, and plays, and holi-
days,*

And hark, away to arms!

And to conquest we will
go! will go! will go!
With the flag of the brave,
To conquest we will go.
A soldier is a gentleman,
  His honor is his life,
And he that won't stand by his flag,
  Will ne'er stand by his wife.

And to conquest we will
go! will go! will go!
With the red, white, and
blue,
To conquest we will go.
For love and honor are the same,
  Or else so ne'er ally'd,
That neither can exist alone,
  But flourish side by side.

And to conquest we will
go! will go! will go!
With the red, white, and
blue,
To conquest we will go.
So fare you well sweethearts awhile,
  You smiling girls adieu,
Ye made this starry flag divine,
  We'll kiss it out with you.

And to conquest we will
go! will go! will go!
With the red, white, and

blue,
To conquest we will go.
The sun is up, our banner shines,
The hills are green and gay,
And all inviting honor calls,
Away! my boys, away!
And to conquest we will
go! will go! will go!
With the red, white, and
blue,
To conquest we will go.
In shady tents by cooling streams,
With hearts all firm and free,
We'll shout the freedom of the land,
In songs of liberty!
And to conquest we will
go! will go! will go!
With the red, white, and
blue,
To conquest we will go.
No foreign slaves shall give us law,
No British tyrants reign,
'Tis Independence made us free,
And Freedom we'll maintain.
And to conquest we will
go! will go! will go!
With the red, white, and
blue,
To conquest we will go.

We'll charge the foe from post to post,
  Attack their works and lines,
And with the stars and stripes aloft,
  We'll capture their Burgoynes.
          And to conquest we will
          go! will go! will go!
          With the red, white, and
          blue,
          To conquest we will go.
And when the war is over, boys,
  Then down we'll sit at ease,
Protected by the freemen's flag,
  And live just as we please.
          When from conquest we
          shall go! shall go! shall go!
          With the red, white, and
          blue,
          From conquest we shall go.
Each hearty lad shall take his lass,
  All beaming like a star,
And in her softer arms forget,
  The dangers of the war.
          When to conquest we did
          go! did go! did go!
          With the red, white, and
          blue,
          To conquest we did go.
The rising WORLD SHALL SING OF
US,

A THOUSAND YEARS *to come,*
And to their children's children tell
The WONDERS WE *have done.*

> *When to conquest we did*
> *go! did go! did go!*
> *With the red, white, and*
> *blue,*
> *To conquest we did go.*

So honest fellows here's my hand,
  My heart, my very soul,
With all the joys of Liberty,
  Good fortune and a bowl.

> *And to conquest we will*
> *go! will go! will go!*
> *With the red, white, and*
> *blue,*
> *To conquest we will go.*

STIRRING APPEALS
FOR CONSTITUTIONAL LIBERTY

"MY LADS, YOU SAY YOU ARE GOING TO FIGHT FOR LIB-erty! these are words in everybody's mouth, but few understand their real meaning. Liberty is not a power to do what we please and have what we desire; this may be the Liberty of a wolf or of a beast of prey, but is not the Liberty of a man considered as a member of society. True Liberty is the being governed by laws of our own making; the inhabitants of every country to choose persons from amongst themselves, in whom they can confide; which persons so elected shall make laws to bind the whole. True Constitutional Liberty is the Liberty for which we are now contending, and may God in his blessings grant this to us all.

"Now, the King of England, has sent over fleets and armies to compel us to give up this invaluable privilege into his hands; but with the blessings of God, we will maintain it against him and all the world, so long as we have a man left to fire a musket. Let our constant prayer be God and Liberty.

"Our Congress have hitherto conducted us with wisdom and integrity, and although in some instances it may be thought they might have managed better than they have done, yet they have piloted us in safety through a tempestuous ocean, to the present period; and so God save the American Congress!"

GEORGE WASHINGTON
THE IDOL OF AMERICA

"MY LADS, I WOULD SPEAK A FEW WORDS OF THE GENeral and his Army, now encamped on the banks of the Schuylkill, enduring all the hardships of their homely situation with cheerful patience; and what is it think you blunts the keen edge of the northern winds, and makes content smile on the tops of frozen hills? I will tell you, it is the love of that 'Liberty' I have sat before you, it is the consciousness of the justice of our cause. I suppose when you think of our incomparable General Washington, you figure to yourselves a stout, bulky man, of a terrible countenance, covered with gold lace, living in a magnificent house and having a great train of attendants around him. You are quite mistaken; he neither has nor needs any external ornaments. Would you hang farthing candles around the Sun to increase his lustre? His glory will admit of no addition. Your General is a plain man, plain in his dress and frugal at his board; yet a native dignity will command your respect, and the affability of his manners win your love. He is brave without ostentation; magnificent without pomp; and accomplished without pride. He is an honor to the human race and the Idol of America. And so God save General Washington and his Army."

THE IMMORTAL FRANCIS SCOTT KEY

ON THE NIGHT OF SEPTEMBER 15, 1814, WHILST THE British fleet, under the command of the English Admiral Cochrane, were bombarding Fort M'Henry, at the city of Baltimore, Francis S. Key, was divinely inspired with the sublime sight of the glorious Banner of the Union still waving over the Fort, and a thousand times reflected, multiplying and increasing in splendor, in every stream of fire throughout the skies, every glare meeting every leaping wave of the billowy Chesapeake Bay, the heavens and waters together joined, each wave glaring with new admired light; but, when the Fort resisted all the efforts of the British ships-of-war, and forced the Admiral to retire, amidst the joyous exultation, the great shouts of the countless hosts of freemen, "Sing ye to the Lord, for he hath triumphed gloriously! The Flag of the Union still triumphs!" Who? Oh! Who can imagine the feelings of Francis S. Key, as o'er his head the flying bombs sang terribly, spent their force in air, and roused all the internal powers of his poetic spirit, his inspired soul to sing still louder?

> *Oh! say can you see by the dawn's early light,*
> *What so proudly we hail'd at the twilight's last gleaming;*
> *Whose broad stripes and bright stars thro' the perilous fight,*
> *O'er the ramparts we watch'd were so gallantly streaming?*
> *And the rockets red glare, and bombs bursting in air,*
> *Gave proof thro' the night that our Flag was still there.*
> *Oh! say does that star spangled*

banner yet wave,
O'er the land of the free and the
home of the brave?
Chorus—
   Oh! say, does the star spangled
   banner yet wave,
   O'er the land of the free and the
   home of the brave?

On the shore dimly seen thro' the
midst of the deep,
Where the foe's haughty host in
dread silence reposes;
What is that which the breeze, o'er
the towering steep,
As it fitfully blows, half conceals,
half discloses?
Now, it catches the gleam of the
morning's first beam,
In full glory reflected now shines in
the stream;
'Tis the star spangled banner, oh!
long may it wave,
O'er the land of the free and the
home of the brave.
Chorus—
   Oh! say, does the star spangled
   banner yet wave,
   O'er the land of the free and the
   home of the brave?

*And where is that band who so
vauntingly swore,
'Mid the havoc of war and the battle's confusion,
A home and a country they'd leave
us no more?
Their blood has wash'd out their
foul footsteps' pollution.
No refuge could save the hireling
and slave,
From the terror of flight, or the gloom
of the grave;
And the star spangled banner in triumph doth wave,
O'er the land of the free and the
home of the brave.
Chorus—*

> *Oh! say, does the star spangled
> banner yet wave,
> O'er the land of the free and the
> home of the brave?*

*Oh! thus be it ever when freemen
shall stand,
Between their loved home and the
war's desolation;
Blest with victory and peace, may
the heaven rescued land,
Praise the Power that made and
preserved us a nation.*

*Then conquer we must, when our
cause it is just,*
*And this be our motto, "In God is
our trust;"*
*And the star spangled banner in tri-
umph shall wave,*
*O'er the land of the free and the
home of the brave.*
Chorus—

  *And the star spangled banner in
triumph shall wave,*
  *O'er the land of the free and the
home of the brave.*

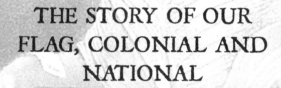

THE STORY OF OUR
FLAG, COLONIAL AND
NATIONAL

Addie Guthrie Weaver

PREFACE

FOR SOME YEARS THE AUTHOR HAS BEEN INTERESTED IN the history of our First Flag and its fair maker, Betsy Ross, and fortunately, through a family relationship with one of the descendants, became familiar with much of the family history.

It seemed that so beautiful and estimable a lady, and one who played so important a part in those stirring events of our early history should be better known and appreciated by her sisters of today.

Fitting, it seems, that while man in defending our Flag has accomplished his greatest achievements, and won undying fame, woman first fashioned into "a thing of beauty" the symbol of that patriotic devotion.

To Mr. George Canby of Philadelphia, and Mrs. Sophia Campion Guthrie of Washington, D. C., grandson and great granddaughter, respectively, of Betsy Ross, the author is indebted for family history that has inspired this work, and to them and other descendants, this book is affectionately dedicated by

THE AUTHOR.

THE STORY OF OUR FLAG
COLONIAL AND NATIONAL

THE HISTORY OF OUR FLAG FROM ITS INCEPTION, IN fact, the inception itself, has been a source of much argument and great diversity of opinion. Many theories and mystifications have gone forth, mingled with a few facts, giving just enough color of truth to make them seem plausible. It is for the purpose of clearing away the veil of doubt that hangs around the origin of the Stars and Stripes that this book has been written.

The Continental Congress in 1775 was very much disturbed over the embarrassing situation of the colonies, and after Washington was appointed Commander-in-Chief of the Army, it showed its independence by appointing a committee composed of Benjamin Franklin, Benjamin Harrison and Mr. Lynch to create a colonial flag that would be national in its tendency. They finally decided on one with thirteen bars, alternate red and white, the "King's Colors" with the crosses of St. Andrew and St. George in a field of blue. The cross of St. Andrew then, as now, was of white, while the cross of St. George was of red. The colonies still acknowledged the sovereignty of England—as this flag attested— but united against her tyranny. This was known as the "flag of our union"—that is, the union of the colonies, and was not created until after the committee had been to the camp at Cambridge and consulted with Washington. It was probably made either at the camp at Cambridge or in Boston, as it was unfurled by Washington under the Charter Oak on January 2, 1776. It received thirteen cheers and a salute of thirteen guns.

It is not known whether Samuel Adams, the "Father of Liberty," was consulted in regard to this flag, but it is a well known fact that he was looking forward, even then, to the independence of the colonies, while Washington, Franklin and the others still looked for justice—tardy though it might be—from England.

Two days later, on the 4th of January, 1776, Washington received the King's speech, and as it happened to come so near to the time of the adoption of the new flag, with the English crosses of St. Andrew and St. George, many of the regulars thought it meant submission, and the English seemed for the time to so understand it; but our army showed great indignation over the King's speech to parliament, and burned all of the copies.

In a letter of General Washington to Joseph Reed, written January 4, he says: "We are at length favored with the sight of his majesty's most gracious speech, breathing sentiments of tenderness and compassion for his deluded American subjects. The speech I send you (a volume of them were sent out by the Boston gentry) was farcical enough and gave great joy to them without knowing or intending it, for on that day (the 2nd) which gave being to our new army, but before the proclamation came to hand, we hoisted the Union flag, in compliment to the United Colonies, but behold it was received at Boston as a token of the deep impression the speech had made upon us and as a signal of submission. By this time I presume they begin to think it strange that we have not made a formal surrender of our lines."

At this time the number and kinds of flags that were in use on land and sea, were only limited to the ingenuity of the state and military officials. This was very embarrassing. On May 20, 1776, Washington was requested to appear before Congress on important secret military business. Major-General Putnam, according to Washington's letters, was left in command at New York during his absence. It was in the latter part of May, 1776, that Washington, accompanied by Colonel George Ross, a member of his staff, and by the Honorable Robert Morris, the great financier of the revolution, called upon Mrs. Betsy Ross, a niece of Colonel Ross. She was a young and beautiful widow, only twenty-four years of age, and known to be expert at needle work. They called to engage her services in preparing our first starry flag. She lived in a little house in Arch street, Philadelphia, which stands to-day unchanged, with the exception of one large window, which has been placed in the front. It was here, in this house, that Washington unfolded a paper on which had been rudely sketched a plan of a flag of thirteen stripes, with a blue field dotted with thirteen stars. They talked over the plan of this flag in detail, and Mrs. Ross noticed that the stars which were sketched were six-pointed, and suggested that they should have five points. Washington admitted that she was correct, but he preferred a star that would not be an exact copy of that on his coat of arms, and he also thought that a six-pointed star would be easier to cut. Mrs. Ross liked the five-pointed star, and to show that they were easily cut she deftly folded a piece of paper and with one clip of her scissors unfolded a perfect star with five points. (See illustration showing the way Betsy Ross folded the paper giving the five-pointed star which has ever since graced our country's banner. A, first fold of a square piece of paper; B, second; C, third, and D, fourth fold. The dotted line AA is the clip of the scissors.)

There is no record that Congress took any action on the national colors at this session,— but this first flag was made by Betsy Ross at this time, and in this way, and we find in Washington's letter of May 28, 1776, to General Putnam at New York, positive instructions "to the several colonels to hurry to get their colors done." In the orderly book, May 31, 1776, are these

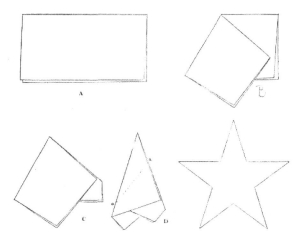

words: "General Washington has written to General Putnam desiring him in the most pressing terms, to give positive orders to all the colonels to have colors immediately completed for their respective regiments." The proof is positive that the committee approved the finished flag of Betsy Ross, and she was instructed to procure all the bunting possible in Philadelphia and make flags for the use of congress, Colonel Ross furnishing the money.

It is easily understood how on account of the meager resources of Congress and the unsettled condition of affairs generally, together with the fact that legislative action was extremely slow and tedious, that Colonel Ross should expedite matters by defraying the expense of this first order for our national colors. There is little, if any, doubt but that Washington on December

24th, Christmas Eve, in 1776, carried the starry flag in making that perilous trip through ice and snow across the Delaware, leading his sturdy, but poorly equipped troops. How inspiring to look back to that night when the Massachusetts fishermen so skilfully managed the boats that the whole army was safely landed and in line of march at four o'clock on Christmas morning. The story of how they plodded on through ice and snow, surprising and defeating the Hessians and capturing a thousand men and their ammunition and equipments, is well known. This was the battle of Trenton, which changed the whole aspect of the war, even causing Lord Cornwallis to disembark and again start in pursuit of Washington, whose cause he had so lately declared lost. It is fitting here to speak of that friend of Washington, Robert Morris, one of the committee that originated our national colors, the great patriot who after the battle of Trenton went from house to house, soliciting money from his friends to clothe and feed this glorious army, which had fought so well.

Congress was very slow to act, and did not seem able to command even the meager resources of the different colonies. It lacked the centralized government which gives it such strength to-day. Considering the grave questions affecting the life and liberty of the people, it is not strange that the flag or any definite action regarding it, was not given prompt consideration. To indicate how slow Congress was to act in regard to the flag, we have only to refer to the Congressional records, which show that the resolution for its adoption was dated over one year after it was actually created, by the committee of which Washington was chief; that is on June 14, 1777. However, a month previous to this, Congress sent Betsy Ross an order on the treasury for £14, 12s. 2d., for flags for the fleet in the Delaware River, and she soon received an order to make all the government flags. The first flag was made of English bunting, exactly the same as those of to-day, excepting that our bunting now is of home manufacture.

There seems to be no question but that these colors, the stars and stripes, were unofficially adopted immediately after the completion of the first flag, the latter part of May, 1776, and that they went into general use at once, so far as it was practicable under the conditions then existing. Washington had the first flag created at this time. It was satisfactory, and he immediately instructed General Putnam to have the colonels prepare their colors—the colors that had just been approved, and which we know to be our flag of to-day.

The first reference we have of an English description of our flag is at the surrender of General Burgoyne, October 17, 1777, when one of the officers said: "The stars of the new flag represent a constellation of states."

Mr. George Canby, an estimable gentleman of the old school, and a grandson of Betsy Ross, has been tireless and indefatigable in his researches on the subject of our flag, and he claims, as did his brother, Mr. William J. Canby, before him, that the first flag with stars and stripes went into immediate use after its inception in the latter part of May, 1776.

The Declaration of Independence was passed by Congress on July 4, 1776, and some authorities, of whom Admiral Preble is the best, seem to infer that the Cambridge flag, with its English crosses, which was unfurled by Washington under the Charter Oak, was still carried by our armies until Congress took action in 1777. That Washington or Congress would sanction the carrying of this flag after the Declaration of Independence seems absurd, and it is certainly against all proof, as well as against the records of the family whose ancestor made the first flag.

Peak's portrait of Washington at the battle of Trenton, December 26 and 27, 1776, shows the Union Jack with the thirteen stars in the field of blue. Admiral Preble says, this is "only presumptive proof" that the stars were at that time in use on our flag, but Titian R. Peale, son of the painter, says: "I visited the Smithsonian Institute to see the portrait of Washington painted by my father after the battle of Trenton. The flag represented has a blue field with white stars arranged in a circle. I don't know that I ever heard my father speak of that flag, but the trophies at Washington's feet I know he painted from the flags then captured, and which were left with him for the purpose." He further says: "He was always very particular in the matters of historic record in his pictures."

This Preble admits in his book, but evidently thought that the artist, Peale, took the flag as it was then (1779), and not the flag of 1776, which the writer claims was identically the same. Through persistent research many facts have come to light that would doubtless have changed the opinion of the late Admiral Preble—facts that were unknown to him.

On Saturday, June 14, 1777, Congress finally officially adopted the flag of our Union and independence, to-wit, resolved, "That the flag of the thirteen United States be thirteen stripes, alternate red and white; that the Union be thirteen stars, white in the blue field, representing a new constellation."

There is not the slightest record in any of the mss. journals in the library of Congress, or in the original files or in the drafts in motions made in the continental Congress of any previous legislative action for the establishment of a national flag for the United States of America, whose independence was declared nearly a year previous. Even after the official adoption of the flag it was not thoroughly brought before the people for many months. All of this adds to the proof that Congress was simply adopting and legalizing a flag that was in general use. That there was no recorded discussion in Congress regarding the adoption of our flag, was perfectly natural, because the star spangled banner came in with our independence, and at this time (June 14, 1777) was simply being officially acknowledged.

There is some diversity of opinion as to how the red, white and blue arranged in the stars and stripes came to be thought of as our flag.

The flag of the Netherlands, which is of red, white and blue stripes, had been familiar to the pilgrims while they lived in Holland, and its three stripes of red, white and blue were doubtless not forgotten. But it seems most probable that the coat of arms of the Washington family furnished more than a suggestion. The coat of arms of his ancestors, that had been adopted by him, comprised the red, white and blue and the stars; and was familiar to all who were associated with Washington. He it was who brought the pencil drawing, when, with the others, he called upon Mrs. Ross to have a suitable flag made, and as we find no mention in history, records or diaries as to who made the drawing, it seems conclusive that he himself designed and drew the plan from his own coat of arms, which was entirely different from England's colors which had become necessarily distasteful.

It seems fitting in this place to write a little history in regard to the Washington coat of arms, the earliest mention of which was by Lawrence Washington, worshipful mayor of Northampton, England, in 1532. In 1540 he placed it upon the porch of his manor house, and on the tomb of Ann, his wife, in 1564. At the old church at Brighton, England, the tombs of Washington's ancestors are marked by memorial plates of brass bearing the arms of the family, which consisted of a shield that bore the stars and stripes. The Archeological Society of England, the highest authority on ancient churches and heraldic matters, states that from the red and white bars, and stars of this shield, and the raven issuant from its crest (borne later by General Washington), the framers of the constitution took their idea of the flag.

When General Washington's great-grandfather, Sir John Washington, came to this country in 1657, the family shield was brought with him.

Sir John settled in Virginia, and established the American line of Washingtons. George Washington afterwards had it emblazoned upon the panels of his carriages, on his watch seals, book marks, and his dishes also bore the same emblem.

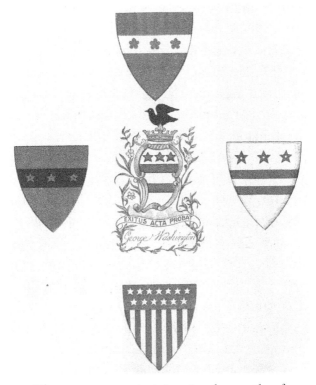

The accompanying image shows the form and colors of the Coat of Arms of the Washington family, back as early as 1300. The name first appeared as De Wessynton; then Weshyngton, and, finally, Washington. How appropriately our own beautiful shield of the United States comes in here, and why not? was he not the "Father of Our Country"? and what more natural than that he should have left the imprint of his life and characteristics in symbol? The central figure is a fac-simile of his book plate.

After the admission of Vermont and Kentucky into the Union, Congress passed an act in 1794, increasing both the stars and stripes from thirteen to fifteen, to take effect May, 1795. It was as follows:

> *An act making alterations in the flag of the United States. Be it enacted, etc., That from and after the first day of May, one thousand, seven hundred and ninety-five, the flag of the United States be fifteen stripes, alternate red and white, and that the union be fifteen stars, white in a blue field.*
>
> *Approved January 13, 1794.*

This flag was used for several years. It flew at the mastheads of our gallant ships and was carried by our little army in the war with England in 1812. A few years later Tennessee, Ohio, Louisiana and Indiana, now won to civilization by hardy pioneers, clamored for admittance into the Union. When they were finally admitted as states, another change in the flag became necessary. The sturdy young republic was ad-

vancing by leaps and bounds in civilization and
wealth; its hardy sons pushing further west and
south constantly, reclaiming from wild savages,
to the uses of their own race, greater and larg-
er areas, which were bound to be erected into
states and take their places in the family of the
original thirteen. It became manifest that legis-
lation was necessary, permanently defining the
national flag, and providing for such changes as
the future development of the country would
require. Congress rose to the occasion. A committee, with Hon. Peter Wendover of New York
as chairman, was appointed to frame a law, and
with very little delay the committee reported a
measure fulfilling every requirement then existing, and providing for all the future. The measure was passed by congress and went on the
statute books as the law establishing the flag as
our great-grandfathers of that day knew it, and
as we know it to-day. The law has never been
changed, and here it is:

> *An act to establish the flag of the
> United States.*
> *Section 1. Be it enacted, etc., That
> from and after the fourth day of July
> next, the flag of the United States be
> thirteen horizontal stripes, alternate
> red and white; that the Union have
> twenty stars, white in the blue field.*

Sec. 2. And be it further enacted, That on the admission of every new state into the Union, one star be added to the union of the flag, and that such addition shall take effect on the fourth of July next succeeding such admission. Approved April 4, 1818.

The thirteen stripes will always represent the number of the "old thirteen" whose patriotism and love of justice brought about the independence of America. The stars that come into the blue sky of the flag will mark or indicate the increase of the states since the adoption of the Constitution. It is interesting to note that under the stars and stripes Washington, in 1793, laid the corner stone of the capitol of the United States, first having personally selected the site of the building. It is also interesting to know that Washington did not live to see the capitol completed, but died before the seat of government was moved to Washington in 1800. The main capitol building was not completed till 1811. It is also a matter of historical interest that the president's home, now called the White House, was completed during the life of Washington, and it is an authenticated fact that he and his wife inspected the house in all its parts only a few days before his death. The president's house was practically destroyed by the British in 1814;

the walls alone remained intact, but the stone was so discolored that when the building was re-constructed, it had to be painted, and from this came the name of the "White House."

The large picture of Washington, by Stewart, which is now in the east room, at the time of the bombardment by the British, was taken out of its frame by Mrs. Dolly Madison, wife of the president, and sent to a secure place across the river.

This flag of forty-five stars, this flag of our country, is our inspiration. It kindles in our hearts patriotic feelings, it carries our thoughts and our minds forward in the cause of liberty and right. On sea and on land, wherever the star spangled banner waves, it thrills the heart of every true American with pride. It recalls the memories of battles bravely fought. It recalls the victories of Trenton and Princeton, it recalls the victories of Gettysburg and Appomattox. We see the flag as first carried by Paul Jones across the sea; we see the flag as carried by Commodore Perry on Lake Erie; we see the flag as carried by Farragut at New Orleans; we see Admiral Dewey through smoke and fire hoisting the flag in the Philippines. This same flag was carried to vic-tory by Admirals Sampson and Schley in Cuba. This flag recalls the many battles bravely fought and grandly won. It symbolizes the principles of human progress and human liberty. The stars represent the unity and harmony of our states. They are the constellation of our country. Their luster reflects to every nation of the world. The flag of 1776, the old thirteen, has grown to be one of the great flags of the earth. Its stars reach from ocean to ocean. We see it leading the armies of Washington and Greene, of Grant and Sherman and Sheridan, and of Miles, Shafter and Merritt.

This is the flag of the "dawn's early light" that was immortalized by Francis Scott Key— "The Star Spangled Banner."

General Grant once said, "No one is great enough to write his name on the flag."

A century under the stars and stripes has been the greatest century of progress in the history of the world. No other nation that has ever existed has carried forward such a banner. Its colors were taken from various sources and brought into one harmonious combination, and it "waves over a country which unites all nationalities and all races, and in the end brings about a homogeneous population, representing the highest type of civilization." It is not strange that this flag of Washington, of Hamilton, of Adams, of Jefferson; this flag of Jackson, of Webster, of Clay, this flag of Lincoln, of Grant and of McKinley should exert such world-wide influ-

ence. It holds a unique place in the nations of
the world. It has spread knowledge and faith and
hope among all classes. It means liberty with
justice. Its international influence places it in
the first rank. It twines itself among the flags of
other nations, not for destruction or war, but for
friendship and progress in the cause of humanity. In the councils of peace; in the conquests of
war; in everything that pertains to government,
in everything that pertains to the advancement
of humanity, it calls forth the admiration of
mankind. Under its influence the arts and sci-
ences have been fostered, commerce has ex-
panded and education has been made univer-
sal. It waves for the right and the harbors of the
globe will salute this banner as a harbinger of
progress and peace.

It is of historical interest that our flag is old-
er than the present flag of Great Britain, which
was adopted in 1801, and it is nine years old-
er than the flag of Spain, which was adopted in
1785. The French tricolor was decreed in 1794;
then comes the flag of Portugal in 1830; then the
Italian tricolor in 1848; then the flags of the old
empires of China and Japan, and of the empire
of Germany, which represents the sovereignty
of fourteen distinct states established in 1870.

Prior to the Revolution, and indeed during
the evolution of a nation through the crucible

of war, separate and distinct flags were popular
with the colonists. Nearly every colony had at
least one. They were not abandoned until it became apparent the colonies were never again to
be colonies, but to form a nation with one flag,
one set of institutions and laws, a fact which inspired the visit of Washington to Betsy Ross as
told in the foregoing papers. Many of the colonial flags were interesting.

GROUP OF COLONIAL FLAGS, No. 1

THE TWO UPPER FLAGS OF THIS GROUP REPRESENT
those used at Bunker Hill July 18, 1775, and
bore these inscriptions: On one side, "An Appeal
to Heaven," and on the other, *"Qui Transtulit
Sustinet"*—He who transported will sustain.

These were beautiful flags, and research
shows that both colors were used. Trumbull
gives the red in his celebrated painting in the
capitol at Washington, and other authentic accounts show that the blue flag was carried also—
the color being the only difference in the two.

THE PINE TREE FLAG

THE PINE TREE FLAG WHICH WAS A FAVORITE WITH THE
officers of the American privateers, had a white
field with a green pine tree in the middle and
bore the motto, "An appeal to heaven."

This flag was officially endorsed by the Mas-

sachusetts council, which in April, 1776, passed
a series of resolutions providing for the regula-
tion of the sea service, among which was the following:

> *Resolved, That the uniform of the of-*
> *ficers be green and white, and that*
> *they furnish themselves according-*
> *ly, and that the colors be a white flag*
> *with a green pine tree and the in-*
> *scription, "An appeal to heaven."—*
> *Harper's Round Table.*

The striped Continental flag opposite the
pine tree flag was of red and white stripes without a field.

THE RATTLESNAKE FLAG

THE DEVICE OF A RATTLESNAKE WAS POPULAR AMONG
the colonists, and its origin as an American emblem is a curious feature in our national history.

It has been stated, that its use grew out of a
humorous suggestion made by a writer in Franklin's paper—the *Pennsylvania Gazette*—that, in
return for the wrongs which England was forc-
ing upon the colonists, a cargo of rattlesnakes
should be sent to the mother country and "distributed in St. James' Park, Spring Garden and
other places of pleasure."

Colonel Gadsden, one of the marine committee, presented to Congress, on the 8th of

February, 1776, "an elegant standard, such as is to be used by the commander-in-chief of the American navy; being a yellow flag with a representation of a rattlesnake coiled for attack."

WASHINGTON LIFE GUARD FLAG

THERE IS PROBABLY NO MORE INTERESTING REVOLUtionary flag than this. The Washington Life Guard was organized in 1776, soon after the siege of Boston, while the American army was encamped near New York.

It was said to have been in the museum at Alexandria, Va., which was burned soon after the war of the rebellion, and nearly everything lost. It was of white silk with the design painted on it.

The uniform of the guard was as follows: blue coat with white facings, white waistcoat and breeches, with blue half gaiters, a cocked hat and white plume.

THE GRAND UNION FLAG

THESE WERE THE COLORS SELECTED BY FRANKLIN, Harrison, and Lynch, and unfurled by Washington under the Charter Oak, January 2, 1776, and hereafter described.

The flag of the Richmond Rifles follows with the one used at Moultrie.

The latter was of blue with white crescent

in the dexter corner and was used by Colonel
Moultrie, September 13, 1775, when he received
orders from the Council of Safety for taking Fort
Johnson on James Island, South Carolina.

In the early years of the Revolution, a number of emblems were in use which became famous. The standard on the southeast bastion of
Fort Sullivan (or Moultrie, as it was afterward

named), on June 28, 1776, by Colonel Moultrie, was a blue flag with a white crescent in the upper left hand corner, and the word "Liberty" in white letters emblazoned upon it.

This was the flag that fell outside the fort and was secured by Sergeant Jasper, who leaped the parapet, walked the whole length of the fort, seized the flag, fastened it to a sponge staff and in sight of the whole British fleet and in the midst of a perfect hail of bullets planted it firmly upon the bastion. The next day Governor Rutledge visited the fort and rewarded him by giving him his sword.

Then comes the flag of White Plains, October 28, 1776, with little historical importance.

The flag made by Betsy Ross, under the direction of General Washington, Robert Morris, and Colonel George Ross, consisted of thirteen bars, alternate red and white, with a circle of thirteen stars in the field of blue.

COUNT PULASKI'S FLAG

THE MORAVIAN SISTERS OF BETHLEHEM, PENNSYLVANIA, gave to Count Pulaski's corps, which he had previously organized at Baltimore and which was called "Pulaski's Legion," a beautiful crimson silk banner, embroidered in yellow silk and sent it with their blessing. Pulaski was at this time suffering from a wound, and was on a visit to Lafayette, whose headquarters were at Bethlehem. Count Pulaski was a Polish patriot, born March 4, 1747. After having bravely fought for Poland with his father and brothers until the Polish cause became hopeless, he came to America, arriving in Philadelphia in 1777. He entered the army as a volunteer, but performing such brave service at Brandywine, he was promoted to the command of cavalry with rank of brigadier-general. In 1778 Congress gave him leave to raise a body of men under his own command. Longfellow has most beautifully described the presentation of the flag in verse. Pulaski bore this flag to victory through many battles until he fell mortally wounded at Savannah, October 14, 1779. The banner was saved by his first lieutenant, who received fourteen wounds, and delivered it to Captain Bentalon, who on retiring from the army, took it home to Baltimore. It was carried in the procession which welcomed Lafayette in 1824, and was then deposited in the Peale Museum. In 1844 Mr. Edmund Peale presented it to the Historical Society of Maryland, where it is now preserved in a glass case. These are interesting historical facts.

Flag of red and blue bars with serpent stretched across and words, "Don't Tread on Me."

Another flag of white, with blue bands top

and bottom and a pine tree in center, with the inscriptions: Liberty Tree and An Appeal to Heaven.

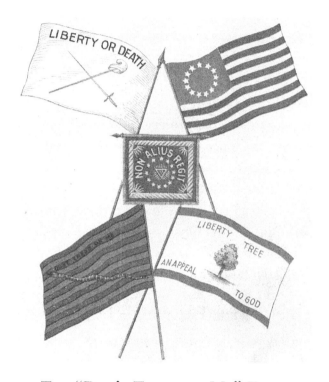

THE "DON'T TREAD ON ME" FLAG

ANOTHER USE OF THE RATTLESNAKE WAS UPON A ground of thirteen horizontal bars alternate red and white, the snake extending diagonally across the stripes, and the lower white stripes bearing the motto—"Don't Tread on Me." The snake was always represented as having thirteen rattles, and the number thirteen seems constantly to have been kept in mind. Thus, thirteen vessels are ordered to be built; thirteen stripes are placed on the flag; in one design thirteen arrows are grasped in a mailed hand; and in a later one thirteen arrows are in the talons of an eagle.

Another "Don't Tread on Me" Flag

One of the favorite flags also was of white with a pine tree in the center. The words at the top were "An Appeal to God," and underneath the snake were the words, "Don't Tread on Me." Several of the companies of minute men adopted a similar flag, giving the name of their company with the motto "Liberty or Death." This flag is familiar to the public as the annual celebrations bring out descriptions of it in the press.

The President's Flag

Within the last few years special flags have been designed for the President, the Secretary of the Navy and Secretary of War. The President's flag is a very beautiful blue banner, in the center of which is a spread eagle bearing the United States shield on its breast, with the thirteen stars in a half circle overhead. It is flown at the main mast-head of naval vessels while the President remains on board, and on being hoisted it is the signal for the firing of the President's salute.

COLONIAL AND PATRIOTIC MUSIC

THE COLONIAL MUSIC WAS MOSTLY BORROWED AND adapted to the occasion. The Pilgrims had more important duties to perform and in those years of stirring events no one was in a mood to write music.

The first song to be used was that old and familiar one, "Yankee Doodle." It made a powerful rallying cry in calling to arms against England. It is so old that it is impossible to decide just where the term came from.

It has been traced back to Greece—*Iank-he Doule*—meaning "Rejoice, O Slave," and to the Chinese—*Yong Kee*—meaning "Flag of the Ocean." It is said the Persians called Americans *Yanki Doon'iah*—"Inhabitants of the New World." The Indians, too, come in for their share of the credit of originating the term, as the Cherokee word *Eankke*, which means "coward" and "slave," was often bestowed upon the inhabitants of New England.

At the time of the uprising against Charles the First, Oliver Cromwell rode into Oxford, on an insignificant little horse, wearing a single plume in a knot called a *macaroni*. The song was sung derisively by the cavaliers at that time. The tune is said to have come from Spain or France, there being several versions of the words.

It came into play when our ancestors flocked

into Ticonderoga in answer to the call of Abercrombie. At that early day no one refused, but all answered the call and came equipped as best they could, but hardly any two alike, and to the trained English regulars must have presented a ridiculous appearance. Dr. Shamburg changed the words of the old satire to fit the new occasion. But in less than a year it was turned by the Yankees against the English in the form of a rallying cry and possessed new meaning.

History had emphasized it, and with the accompaniment of the shrill pipe and half worn drum calling the simple cottagers together, it must have aroused all their noble and sturdy patriotism.

Who that has viewed that stirring picture in the Corcoran Art Gallery at Washington, "Yankee Doodle," could fail to catch the inspiration of the scene. The old man with his thin grey locks, but head erect and face glowing with enthusiasm as he keeps time to the old tune, followed by the small boy with his drum. One scarcely knows whether humor or pathos predominates: but certain we are that all alike stepped to its chords; it found an answering echo in each heart and led them on to glory.

"Yankee Doodle"

Father and I went down to camp.
Along with Captain Goodwin,

And there we saw the men and boys
As thick as hasty pudding.
CHORUS.
Yankee Doodle, keep it up.
Yankee doodle dandy;
Mind the music and the step.
And with the girls be handy.
And there was Captain Washington,
Upon a slapping stallion.
A giving orders to his men.
I guess there was a million.—Cho.
And then the feathers on his hat.
They looked so tarnal finey,
I wanted peskily to get
To give to my Jemima.—Cho.
And there they had a swamping gun.
As big as a log of maple,
On a duced little cart,
A load for father's cattle.—Cho.
And every time they fired it off
It took a horn of powder;
It made a noise like father's gun,
Only a nation louder.—Cho.
I went as near to it myself
As Jacob's underpinin',
And father went as near again,
I th't the duce was in him.—Cho.
It scared me so, I ran the streets,
Nor stopped as I remember,

Till I got home and safely locked
In granny's little chamber.—Cho.
And there I see a little keg.
Its heads were made of leather;
They knocked upon it with little
sticks
To call the folks together.—Cho.
And then they'd fife away like fun
And play on corn-stalk fiddles;
And some had ribbons red as blood
All bound around their middles.—
Cho.
The troopers, too, would gallop up,
And fire right in our faces;
It scared me almost to death
To see them run such races.—Cho.
Uncle Sam came there to change
Some pancakes and some onions,
For 'lasses cake to carry home
To give his wife and young ones.—
Cho.
But I can't tell you half I see,
They keep up such a smother:
So I took off my hat, made a bow,
And scampered off to mother.—Cho.

AMERICA

REV. SAMUEL FRANCIS SMITH WAS BORN IN BOSTON
October 21, 1808, and graduated in the class

of '29 from Harvard University. He enjoyed the honor of having for his classmate Oliver Wendell Holmes, in whose beautiful poem, entitled "The Boys," the name of the author of "America" is affectionately mentioned.

> *And there's a nice youngster of excellent pith;*
> *Fate tried to conceal him by naming him Smith.*
> *But he shouted a song for the brave and the free,*
> *Just read on his medal—"My Country of Thee"!*

"America" was written in 1832, the tune being the old one of "God Save the Queen," and first rendered on the 4th of July of the same year by the children of Park St. Church, Boston.

"America"

> *My country, 'tis of thee,*
> *Sweet land of liberty,*
> *Of thee I sing!*
> *Land where my fathers died,*
> *Land of the pilgrims' pride,*
> *From every mountain side*
> *Let freedom ring.*
> *My native country, thee—*
> *Land of the noble free,*
> *Thy name I love.*
> *I love thy rocks and rills,*

Thy woods and templed hills.
My heart with rapture thrills
Like that above.
Let music swell the breeze
And ring from all the trees
Sweet Freedom's song!
Let mortal tongues awake,
Let all that breathe partake,
Let rocks their silence break,
The sound prolong.
Our fathers' God, to thee,
Author of Liberty!
To Thee we sing:
Long may our land be bright
With freedom's holy light,
Protect us by Thy might,
Great God, our king!

Peace follows where it finds the Old Thirteen, the nucleus around which the other stars have gathered in their glory.

—Letitia Green Stevenson, Honorary Vice President General National Society, Daughters of the American Revolution.

THE OLD THIRTEEN
A PATRIOTIC SONG DEDICATED TO THE SONS, DAUGHTERS AND CHILDREN OF THE AMERICAN REVOLUTION

1. Flag of the free, we hail thee with pride.

Float thou in freedom o'er all the land wide;

Emblem of pow'r where'er thou art seen. Yet

still we are true to The Old Thirteen.

Our fathers who fought a free country to make.

Who suffered and died for sweet liberty's sake.

What joy had been theirs had they only foreseen

How vast we should grow from The Old Thirteen—

Forty-five stars now shine in thy blue,

Forty-five states to thee will be true—

As heroes of old keep their memory green.

Who marched with the flag of The Old Thirteen.

2. We'll work for thy glory forever and aye.

We'll celebrate ever that dearly bought day;

Thy folds floating o'er us in triumph were seen,

So valiantly won by The Old Thirteen.

*We'll rally around thee from near
and from far,
Our standard forever in peace or in
war,
All nations salute thee, thy stars'
mighty sheen,
Full splendor thou art of The Old
Thirteen.
Then hail we our emblem, each
daughter and son,
Honor the vict'ry thy fair folds have
won;
Tho' multiplied stars float in free-
dom serene,
Enshrined in our hearts is The Old
Thirteen.*

Words by Corrilla Copeland Lewis
Music by Harriet Hayden Hayes.

STARS ON THE FLAG

THE HOME MAGAZINE CONTAINS THE FOLLOWING BEAU-
tiful suggestion regarding the placing of the stars
on the flag:

Number 1 is the field of our first stars and
stripes made by Betsy Ross.

Number 2 represents that field of flag of 1814
which inspired the "Star Spangled Banner."

Number 3 the field of 1818 designed by Capt.
S. C. Reid.

Number 4, field of our present flag.

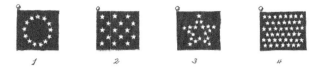

Although there is no law saying who shall arrange the stars on our flag, or how they shall be arranged, it is customary for the changes to be made in the war department when new states have been admitted to the Union.

The incongruous variations in figures A, B, C, which are reproductions of unions taken from new flags, made by different manufacturers, would not exist if there was a law fixing the arrangement of the stars.

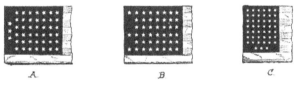

It is believed by many that the stars on our flag should be arranged into a permanent and symmetrical form, fixed by law, instead of the present changeable and uncertain form, which is subject in a great measure, to the caprice or convenience of the flag maker. It is not generally known that among the many flags in use in our country to-day, there is an utter lack of uniformity in the arrangement of the stars.

In the selection of a form, three different

things should be considered—its historical significance, symmetry, and adaptability. The stars should be so arranged that it will not be necessary to make any noticeable change when new ones are added. The stars should always remain equal in size, representing the equality of the states.

In the form which is submitted, No. 8, with the group of thirteen stars in the center, representing the thirteen original states, they are arranged in exactly the same form as they appear on the great seal of the United States. The circle containing twenty-three stars, represents the states which were admitted to the Union up to the close of the civil war. These two features are symbolic of the two great events in the nation's history—the one which brought our flag into existence, and the other which made its life permanent by welding the sisterhood of states into a perfect and indestructible union. The circle is also symbolic of unity, peace, and preservation.

The outside circle of nine stars, represents the states which have been added to the Union since the civil war. New stars can be added to this circle without changing the symmetry of the arrangement, as will be seen by reference to the illustration. As this circle will always remain an open one, there will always be room for one more star, and it is thus significant of progression.

One great advantage in this form is, that it is suggestive of a constellation, and thus carries out, as far as practicable, the idea of the framers of the resolution of 1777 in establishing the flag.

John F. Earhart is the author of the above description of the different forms of flags.

THE LIBERTY CAP

THE HISTORIANS WHO HAVE SEARCHED THE ARCHIVES of ancient and medieval times tell us that this has been a symbol of liberty since the Phrygians made the conquest of the eastern part of Asia Minor.

After the conquest they stamped it on their

coins, and to distinguish themselves from the primitive peoples they used the liberty cap as a head dress. The Romans used a small red cap called a "pileus," which they placed on the head of a slave in making him free, and when Caesar was murdered a Phrygian cap was carried through the streets of Rome proclaiming the liberty of the people. The liberty cap of the English is blue with a white border.

It remained for the United States to adopt the British cap, adding to it the crescent of thirteen stars. Generals Lee and Schuyler, with the Philadelphia Light Horse troop, adopted it in 1775. This is the famous troop that escorted Washington to New York.

It is most familiar to us as seen on our coins, on which it was first used after the Revolution as a symbol of freedom.

Edward Everett Hale, in one of his impressive orations, says: "The starry banner speaks for itself; its mute eloquence needs no aid to interpret its significance. Fidelity to the Union blazes from its stars; allegiance to the government beneath which we live is wrapped in its folds."

The Stars and Stripes was officially first unfolded over Ft. Schuyler, a military port in New York state, now the city of Rome, Oneida county. It was first saluted on the sea by a foreign power, when floating from the masthead of the *Ranger*,

Capt. Paul Jones commanding, at Quiberon Bay, France, February 14, 1778. The salute was given by Admiral La Motte, representing the French government.

The first vessel over which the Union flag floated was the ship *Ranger*, built at Portsmouth, New Hampshire, whose gallant commander was the famous Paul Jones.

Its first trip around the world was on the ship *Columbia*, which left Boston September 30, 1787, commanded by Captains Kendrick and Gray. It was three years then in circling the globe. Today it waves in every clime, on every sea.

It is pleasing to note how Franklin, when minister to France, secured the ship *Doria* from the French and gave to Paul Jones the command, who immediately renamed the old ship "Bon homme Richard," in honor of Franklin.

ORIGIN OF "OLD GLORY"

THE TERM OLD GLORY IS SAID TO HAVE BEEN ORIGI-nated by an old sailor—Stephen Driver.

While upon the seas he performed an act of bravery for which he was rewarded by the gift of an American flag, whereupon he pledged its givers to always defend it faithfully.

At the outbreak of the civil war he was living in Nashville, Tenn. In order to keep the flag safely he concealed it in a bed-quilt under which he slept. To the enemies of the Union he declared that Old Glory would yet float from the staff of the Tennessee state house, and sure enough when Nashville fell into the hands of Gen. Buell he secured the flag from its hiding place and hoisted it to a more fitting position on the state house—thus his nick-name for it became popular.

JOHN JAY AT MOUNT KISCO
JULY 4, 1861

HE SAID, "SWEAR ANEW AND TEACH THE OATH TO OUR children, that with God's help the American Republic shall stand unmoved though all the powers of piracy and European jealousy should combine to overthrow it. That we shall have in the future as we have had in the past, one country, one constitution, one destiny; and that when we shall have passed from earth, and the acts of to-day shall be matters of history, and the dark power which sought our overthrow shall have been overthrown, our sons may gather strength from our example in every contest with despotism that time may have in store to try their virtue, and that they may rally under the Stars and Stripes with our old time war cry, "'Liberty and Union, now and forever, one and inseparable.'"

UNCLE SAM

THIS TERM ORIGINATED AT THE TIME OF OUR WAR WITH England in 1812. Provisions were purchased at Troy, N. Y., and the agent was Elbert Anderson, the work being superintended by Ebenezer and Samuel Wilson, the packages being marked E. A. U. S. Samuel Wilson was known all over as Uncle Sam and he was often joked about his amount of provisions, then the newspapers took it up and the term Uncle Sam came into general use and is typical of our increasing national prosperity. Quite recently a portrait of an actual personage whose features are identical with those made familiar by caricatures of Uncle Sam, was found in possession of a family near Toledo, Ohio. The portrait was painted about 1818, but nothing is known of the shrewd, kindly old man represented. His face was undoubtedly the origin of the accepted caricature.

BROTHER JONATHAN

JONATHAN TRUMBULL, GOVERNOR OF CONNECTICUT, was a warm friend of General Washington, who had great confidence in his judgment.

When in need of ammunition and the question arose as to where they could get the necessary means for defense Washington said: "We will consult Brother Jonathan."

After that whenever they needed help the

expression became a common one and naturally came to mean the United States Government.

THE AMERICAN EAGLE

OUR BALD HEADED EAGLE, SO CALLED BECAUSE THE feathers on the top of the head are white, was named the Washington eagle by Audubon. Like Washington it was brave and fearless, and as his name and greatness is known the world over, so the greatest of birds can soar to the heights beyond all others.

In 1785 it became the emblem of the United States.

It is used on the tips of flag staffs, on coins, on the United States seals, and on the shield of liberty.

BANNERS AND STANDARDS

IT IS NOT GENERALLY KNOWN THAT THE TASSELS WHICH are pendent customarily from the upper part of banners and standards, and the fringe which surrounds them are relics of the practice of observing sacred emblems. They originated in pagan devices and the garments of priests and were consecrated to specific forms of worship.

Sacred history is full of instances of the consecration of tassels and peculiar fringes to special sacerdotal uses. Blue was early the emblem of purity and innocence and that fact accounts for the predominance of that color in the ecclesiastical badges of these early times. When the use of the tassels passed into profane customs, they were used as ornaments for national standards and for royal girdles, and it was not infrequent that they were first blessed by the priests. It has followed naturally that this use has continued up to the present time, although now it is retained probably because of the artistic effect of the swinging pendants.

THE LINCOLN FLAG
PRESENTED BY THE FRENCH PEOPLE

THE FLAG IN THE WHITE HOUSE WHICH FORMERLY hung in the center of the largest window in the east room, has a unique history.

It is woven of silk in one piece without a seam. There are gold stars in the field and among them are seen the words in French, "Popular subscription to the Republic of the United States, offered in memory of Abraham Lincoln. Lyons, 1865."

STATE FLAGS

AS THE COLONIES HAD THEIR FLAGS OF DIFFERENT kinds so the states one by one adopted special flags and nearly all the states of the Union now have a state flag or regimental color. In some states this emblem is established by law, in other versal extension throughout Christendom.

In time the Crown assumed this protective power, and the phrase was changed to "La paix et la treve du Roi," or "The peace and truce of the king." The republics recognized the time-honored institution, and the simple unfolding of a white cloth will instantly cause a cessation of hostilities. The adoption of a white emblem appears to be lost in tradition, as authorities do not reveal it. Doubtless it is similar, or may have arisen through a belief in the white Samite which shielded the Holy Grail from the gaze of unbelievers. Emblematic of purity, associated with the mythical knights of the Round Table, and used in the Crusades, it is probable that this sacred truce flag may have originated from the Samite of the Holy Grail.

At the present time, if presented during an engagement firing is not required to cease; nor, if the bearer be killed or wounded, is there ground for complaint. The truce emblem can be retained if admitted, during an engagement. Penalties are incurred if the truce emblem be wrongfully used, the severest being the ignominious death of a spy.

THE BON HOMME RICHARD FLAG

THIS HISTORIC OLD FLAG, ALSO KNOWN AS THE PAUL Jones Flag, composed of thirteen bars and but twelve stars, was unfurled by him and borne on the Bon Homme Richard September 23, 1776, during the action with the British frigate, the "Serapis," and is probably the first flag bearing the stars and stripes ever hoisted over an American vessel of war, and also the first ever saluted by a foreign naval power.

This flag has been in the family of Mrs. H. R. P. Stafford, of Cottage City, Martha's Vineyard, since 1784, and bequeathed by her to the National Museum at Washington.

But it must be remembered that Washington adopted the flag made by Betsy Ross five months previous to this.

BIRTH OF OUR NATION'S FLAG

THE FIRST AMERICAN FLAG ACCEPTED by COMMITTEE and ADOPTED by Resolution of Congress JUNE 14th, 1777, as the National Standard, was made by BETSEY ROSS in 1776, at 239 Arch Street, Philadelphia, in the room represented in this picture. The Committee ROBERT MORRIS and Hon. George ROSS, accompanied by GENERAL GEORGE WASHINGTON, called upon this Celebrated Woman, and, together with her suggestions, produced our beautiful EMBLEM OF LIBERTY.

"How Betsy Made the Flag" (excerpt)

Said Washington to Betsy Ross,
"A flag our nation needs
To lead our valiant soldiers on
to high and noble deeds
Now can you make one for us,
to which she made reply,
"I am not certain if I can; At
least I'll gladly try."
So she took some red for the blood they shed
Some white for purity,
Some stars so bright from the sky overhead
Some blue for loyalty,
And sewed them all together,
For loyal hearts and true,
And hand in hand as one we stand
For the red, the white and the blue.
Said Betsy Ross to Washington,
"Your country's flag behold!"
And through his tear-dimmed eyes he
saw the stars and stripes unfold.
Then to his breast he clasped it,
and looked to heaven above.
"Oh may it ever stand," he cried,
"For rights and truth and love."

— *C. Austin Miles*

RECIPE FOR SUCCESS: FIND GREAT BOOKS AND READ THEM.

#ReadSucceedBeautiful

If You Enjoyed
This Book
Then You'll Also Enjoy…

The first – and only – traditionally published book by the legendary Five Hundred Million Dollar Man, J.F. (Jim) Straw, whose business activities have generated over $500,000,000 in revenues. In *Mustard Seeds, Shovels, & Mountains*, Mr. Straw explains how he used what he calls "Physio-Psychic Power" to achieve such incredible success.
A #1 Best Seller on Amazon.com!

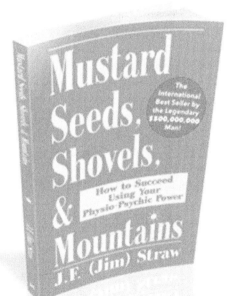

"Anyone who wants to improve their position, succeed at their dreams, truly help others, etc. needs to READ THIS BOOK!!! (sorry to shout, but I really feel this way.)"
–Amazon.com Reviewer

10% OFF YOUR NEXT BOOK!
Use Coupon Code: **BETSY2019**

www. **ALLISTI**publishing.com

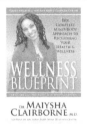

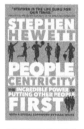

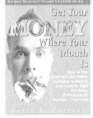

Made in the USA
Coppell, TX
09 January 2024

27482182R00056